Poems for My Wife

Poems, Songs and Love Notes

for Abigail Lewis

Michael Louis Mollo

SYCAN PRESS

Poems for My Wife
by Michael Louis Mollo
© 2020 Michael Louis Mollo

Published by
Sycan Press, Ashland, Oregon

Book design: booksavvystudio.com
Cover photography by Michael Louis Mollo
Author photo by Abigail Lewis

ISBN: 978-0-578-64294-9
First Edition
Printed in the United States of America

Dedication

My dearest Abigail Lewis,
you are my true love.
This book is, of course,
dedicated to you.
Happy birthday.
Within these pages are
some of the many poems, songs and love notes
I have written to you over the past fifteen years.
There are so many more.
Also, I have included poems
inspired by you
that address my personal struggles
and concerns for society.
Thank you, sweet one,
for seeing me through.
I love you.
God bless you.
Faithfully yours forever,

Michael Louis Mollo

Contents

Poems for My Wife

Preface

Devotional and experimental, this collection of poetry offers an intimate view into the lives of a faithful couple struggling with the poet's madness eventually overcome through expression of love. Mostly free verse and haiku, the book includes poems composed when the author was in the throes of a prolonged psychotic paroxysm, and poems for the woman who healed him.

Tanka 35

I watch your profile
show in subtle ways a joy
that is the force born
to open stars in the dark
as we share another sigh.

I was so happy to see you I forgot
to give you a love note:
I love you!!!

Styx-Raft

Find me
in cool stillness
find me
beyond abyss

I've thrown the TV
out of the loft
I dance alone
slow and soft

Snuff out
the city's static hiss
Come closer sis
look at this

still closer
sis
look at
this

I love you.

The Gramercy of
Arrow Ganjol

Indigo flowers become the twilight gale
where crossed stalks loosen into rune
and the old rock holds

a desperado's sudden benediction
strobing in revenant aria
until the lightning leaves the field

An old sarod in soft stature is sweetening
cafe voice composure
and again I must leave

A perfect thank you eagers for the eagle
of your voice where the thresholding
penumbra heraldry is fire

Because of your unrepentant stylus
and your field of yielding
I staved off

multiplying heads
of the lusus naturae
in my day

This nod a heroine shout out
an unfurling from the uninhibited
amorphous ocean of one solitary whisper

A blue anomaly this lightning-glassed sand
interred for the fist of an ensphering eon
unearthed now in seeing you well

Your words are as waves
and how could one man standing on night
shore alone with arms wide

conceive to hold back the sea's
unceasing
refrain

The textures your feet have felt
inside the poppy
on the star

are not mine
as I fumble in city firmament
as I rumble in regal sylvan wilderness for it

I see you enough to protect you entirely
and effortlessly intone the portent
we ride through rain bareback

Without crowing unkindness this last Old
Gold smoke is chivalrously offered
from the pack in boots and black

You

Abigail's Sonnet

Forty seasons with you, my precious love,
have given me stature and character
in a dimension of light that will move
forever forward with grace. Protector
of you, my precious love, I am always.
Crimson-purple mountains bloom slowly like
The Universal Tree itself. Sun rays
and waves of starlight, and the moon: a haik,
a tapestry of love for unfurling
forms, for terrestrial textures, for life.
Unending, I meet your smile in morning
promise and benevolence, you, my wife.
Woven around our union are great streams
of incense, symphonies, and sacred dreams.

I love you with my
whole being.

Untitled

First
face the showdown
with the shadow

then choose
your cup
of joy

It is like this
two roads
one

is gratitude
the other
hunger

In the United States
of Thanksgiving
he is free

to pluck among
a multitude
of amenities

he is aware enough
to refine his
character

he has the power
to avoid anyone
who has no star

no original discipline
(eyes
of dull black

stone
loose and predatory
in a mediocre arena)

Shunka Tanka Wakan
devour this
wasichu disease

Ma Dawg
 I am
a nation

Mitakuye Oyasin

Walking with You

Reaching a stature
of still trees

for heights of day
and deeps of night,

great spectrums
of pure starlight.

The serene and sirened forest
sentinels around an ancient

wildflower
dancing

subtle and thrilling
tales of being

for a stature of trees
still reaching.

Abigail,
I have a profound amount
of respect for you. You
are always threading miracles
for so many people.
I love you.
— Michael

Oasis

I

Sun
and skull in desert.

II

Drifting,
thinking

these ex-impressions
deserve the world

and the world
these.

III

How shallow
I've been

assuming I understand
things

upon standard consideration.
"Right."

Twin Flame

Your diamond smile
glowing with celestial light:
sun on sunflowers.

I LOVE

Your eyes
Your face
Your smile
Your voice
Your body
Your___s
Your laugh
Your ideas
Your gifts
Your thoughtfulness
Your compassion
Your firmness
Your greatness
 You

Michael + Abigail
= Heart

Asceticism

Asleep in the woods,
dreaming of meditating.
Woodpecker knocks twice.

There is no 'man versus nature',
there is only nature.

Wild Law

No known beginning
to integrity unbroken,
to sand and rain.

Broken ships at sea
crack and laugh while
the night observes a split-toothed

sailor honoring his word
to not slander the captain
while unsteady with intoxication.

Thick with battle wounds and
martyrdom repose, he owes
not, nor woes the pain to not

let his honor go;
he owes not but chooses a dignity
with no known beginning.

Abigail,

How I love you forever...
How do I say?
How?

— Michael

The Innocent Savagery of Love

We were turned on
by one another.

We dove into
and mutually devoured at

the delight, the
desire.

Like black widow spiders
leathered and erotic

in spectacular stillness,
you strike at what you like.

We came
to each other

as magnetic fire,
fierce howling plumages

of flame, red and black,
ecstatic and immortal.

*Have a
Happy Day!*

Anew

Your innocence is pure
and I am now anew,
certain your soul knows
I am sorry.

I was a thousand ghosts
begirding a beggar's dark bird
leave the green for madness
in a sanguine pastoral.

Sheets ghettoed my windows
while sticks vetoed the door
through a prolonged clawing
effrontery of apocalypse night.

We smoked stolen grit
for the viola asylum's venom
while Venus steered
the chalky crescent down.

Larrup voices shriveled
into dancing mirrors
slinging transverse versions
of pinecones boiling

in neon sand
until a weak temerity held
onto the trajectory
of equivocal corporeal defeat.

I awoke in the ICU
to seven orderlies
floating my bones in ketamine
at frosted sunrise.

I don't recall it
or my seizure
in the long loud box
of a Charon ambulance.

But I fear I hurt you
knowing less than what you intended.
Widowed ash from my brow
returns to you.

Remain strong,
my true love,
looking above the lake
and these broken brushstrokes.

See me anew.
I kicked through weeks of sweat
and dessicated, fissured fingers
burning into this.

A -

Soup is Great!

DYKHMILY? MTT.
— M

Would You

pour your blood back
into
The Earth
solely
to nourish
a wilting bamboo,
a withering weed,
a healthy one?

Fake Nature?
Lawn for cement
Law enforcement

Bloodline

Royalty is a sickness
of non-compassion
and ostentatious display

The blood of Nature
is not a myth
nor is it rancid with tyranny

Ask the tiger if he likes the cage
Ask the people if they love the royal elite
Ask yourself

what you would give
of yourself
when naked in the wild

while our tigress hungers
yet still gives suck
to the cubs she loves

Abigail,

I Love
You
Forever.

— Michael

Birch

Purity
Renewal

I love you.
Have a GREAT day,
Abigail Lewis

— Michael

I LOVE YOU!

*What a great
friend, lover,
wife, you are - so
beautiful, so full
of rich and sweet
graceful creativity.*

*All my love,
— Michael*

What is Truth?

Silence.

Pain.

Love.

Abigail,
Your smile...
Thank you, my wife. I love you.

— Michael

Your true, faithful and
eternal husband.

Caniculares

Stray dogs ululate
from agora alleyways.
Sirius ascends.

wLOVEs

Living It

You can't fake
an abounding life
with contrived words.

After you've lived
masterfully for long enough
that it is now your natural self,

you can begin
to write poetry
that sparks something of awe.

If you can pull together
a personal grace with grit,
you've got something.

The manipulation
of formulaic wordcraft
is fun to puzzle together,

but by itself
is facile and fleeting
to a reader.

There has to be the strength
of original rebellion
behind it.

Being coddled by an opulent norm
for a vain impetus
makes for a boring writer.

Formal schooling alone
is too commonplace
a homogeneity

to be an attractive achievement
for the real adventuring
human soul.

There must be action, ingenuity,
beyond the pandered-for safety
of stereotypical entertainment.

What makes a writer
a value to a reader
is introspective solitude

and a wherewithal
developed by the resourcefulness
derived from poverty

and various exile.
Battles won, or at least survived,
when alone with life

are what season
the prospective
writer.

A plethora of kowtowing
to the unexamined
and unchallenged

empire of the day does little
to approach the preservable word.
Foolishness is not the way either.

It is wise and strategic risk
that brings about
a compelling story.

Blessings, Love.

Abigail

(written from jail)

Angel of righteous light,
goddess of mysterious, exuberant might,
woman of eternal incandescent innocence—
oh, how I love you, my Abigail Lewis.

"A blessing of tea," you said
while twirling with a cup and spilling some.
Enchanted, I proposed a walk on high.
You accepted, we excited at adventure.

We are one:
you, all the goodness of the world in the wilderness—
me, wild in a world starved for justice.
Through streets of graceful chaos,

your smile, your smile…

Abigail,

I Love You.

—Michael

Refractory

Flying on the ground,
defying all droll dogma:
butterfly shadow.

Nothing likes a cage.

Forever
(written from jail)

Abigail Lewis,
recall our words
in the hot springs
at Dark Hollow.

My one twin flame,
this majestic light
is wild
and sweet to follow.

My only soul mate,
I'll chase you
through forests
of Isis and Apollo.

My dear, dear love,
a pure white dove
from the heart
of Michael Louis Mollo.

Dinner 4 U in Fridge.
I Love You.

—M

Nations

A
woman
spoke:

"The image of The Divine
is not human, it is Life
which includes human beings;

it is certainly
not the blind folly
of elitist arrogance.

The truth sits there like a mountain
whether one believes in something
more convenient or not.

Versions are not the original nor
The Creator
of origins.

We are just
one nation of lifeforms
created among many."

The
Heavens
agreed.

A Light Rain

A light rain
approaching stillness

in its apparency
is for my walk

through this
forested town.

I think of you,
my true love,

as pure waters,
as the wilderness water

that no one else sees
moving over dark rocks

beneath a poised living canopy.
Many faces see you,

adore you,
in the swirling cities.

I do.
Yet I feel you deeper

in the way
we call sacred.

I recognize your movements
as the water of the wild

for mosses
and trees bending or reaching,

the deer that dips its head momentarily,
a changing cloud, this rain.

My spirit is touched
by the truth

of your everlasting majestic grandeur
and peace.

Abigail,

I LOVE YOU!
I am @ Guru Vey.
Would love to see you.
The Earth is
Heart
  or
Hearth
YOU

—Michael

Blue Fire

Abigail you gunna stay long lay around
Love on me until you tire
If that spirit come to haunt me down send it out
I'm stayin' here right by your blue fire

Children dance and sing across the lake
Old volcano's about to quake out the ache
Do what you gotta do and higher
I'm stayin' here right by your blue fire

Abigail,

I am so proud of you.
I love and support you,
my precious love. Peace.

—Michael

Dragon Book Poems

Where are they?
Where is that red leather book
with two dragons facing each other
embossed on the cover?

There are poems in there
that would make a dark desert incandescent,
words that would diaphanously
end all imperial menageries.

The animals
would then roam the land
looking for their respective temples
and the two lover

dragons
who
freed
them.

Abigail Hi

<u>I LOVE YOU!</u>
Have a good day.

—Michael

About as Honest as
I Can Be:

I am by nature and circumstance
a very angry and passionate man,
yet tender like anyone.
I find that the loving touch
of my wife brings me great peace.
I know I am here for her.
I am <u>not</u> destructive when in
that safe, loving space of her embrace.
I am her husband, protector and beast,
yet I am often frightened, alone,
and destructive when I fear betrayal
because I have been betrayed by people.
I have been hurt physically and institutionalized
to the point of panic and trauma.
I am not a victim but as well
I feel safe in Abby's strong embrace
like she does in mine.

—Michael

Abigail
Lewis,
Mollo
Loves
You...

One Moon Cycle

My love,
we were born
exactly one moon cycle apart.

I came into the world first
to make sure all would be safe
for you.

I am twenty-eight days your elder
this time around
but you have been my elder in the past,

I am sure,
and you'll be it again in the future,
and I yours.

So I have no stage for smugness,
only an everlasting
diamond bowl

for our remarkable
marital martial art, and our
celestial sugar.

Abigail,

I love you! I am so very proud of you!
I am glad you are succeeding!

—Michael

Two Hours Passing

Sage smoke rolls up
red ribbons waving
to those ghosted in rapture-arrest
like rocks aware and drawing one divine breath.

Through the emerald limen,
every form of beauty is untouched
as the scene of one's life passing
passes.

Waters carry by.
The bright flower disinters
from mossy cracks on the day we ourselves
unlace back into her breast.

A distant vision
of when we were beautiful
breaks,
and we stop,

for what we are
is what we thought
we could never be,
and what we will never be again.

Abigail,
Have a righteousness.
—Michael
I LOVE YOU

Swaraj

I

Swaraj, mountain of the world,
author of eclipse and authentic renewal,
seer of celestial proving and encircled
approximation,
ensphering even these orbital auguries,
is august by itself.

Fury for justice explodes in each cell of the
body, individually.
A billion religions bow inward toward an
enigmatic omnipotence unseen by all.
"Do you like the tables arranged like this?"
asks a woman with a coy head-tilt side-glance.

Hat-stance staunch-man
reads from his pepper and thyme-scented
green leather grimoire.
Unfurling from the feral garden,
another set of sentient eyes open.

To practice self-restraint and simplicity,
to embrace a personal longsuffering with
measured discipline, to endure
empowerment through hard exertion,
is the true expansion.

II

I saw Saturn rising orange on a desolate
horizon.
The reeds and serrated grasses rose to
refine me.
The hunger at neon
city-edge was an establishment
of self-manifestation, of swaraj.

"Look this way," said Gladys Pillgrim.
Gladys Pillgrim was, at times, a cacophony
of orchestrated
anti-order; a distorted guitar without
its velvet caress;
a cocoon of hats, all assembled by the capricious
guest of indifference.

"Look again," she said. Then, "Look again."
She experimented with pixelated mentors,
some demonstrating the application of
whale-corpse makeup,
some encouraging entrepreneurship,
some shooting at en vogue entropy
through apathy.

This contains something vain.
This contains something vague.
This contains something vogue.
This contains something rogue.
This contains some rain.

"What music is this?" asked Wally Four Feathers.
He was referring to the referee,
the innocent-eyed dimebag of dirt
playing at pitying
while eating all the snacks.

Four Feathers met Pillgrim and vomited.
The music stopped.
The gunfire stopped.
"When it comes down to it, it is all friendly fire,"
said Four Feathers.

"Red is the old Red," he added.
"Wally Four Feathers, get ye to a dinner party
from the nineteen-fifties," screamed
Gladys Pillgrim.
Birds of a dulled shale color emerged
from a dark green bush
and their wings made a drumroll sound.

III

"I've never been to an event like this,"
said Monad.
Monad was sensitive.
People had to be careful around him
so he could advance his agenda,
or so he stealthily insisted.

Tall birds joined the ranks. Their stripes revealed
that they justified eating veal via big smiles.
Other birds not fond of ballroom dancing
felt ashamed

to address Monad's burgeoning aggression
and worship of the number language.

"I will not tell," spoke Clarabell.
She liked watching the nameless tall birds
even though some of them beat other
smaller birds
with their clumsy wings when flying to the
billboard trough.
"I will tell with my poses," clarified Clarabell.

"Shut up," said Monad. "You ain't goin'
nowhere."
The wind picked up a high school cheat sheet,
read it, and then flippantly flipped it
out of its invisible tentacles.
"Nowhere."

"I've seen better days… when I was exiting and
entering
Greyhound buses," said Clarabell, looking down
at her flip-flops and opining about
her own life in a half-certain, maudlin way.
Milk came raining down from the fourteenth
floor of a nearby skyscraper.

The crew shooed themselves from the scene
collectively
but each with individual fears.
They ran.
The milk stopped.
Then the real rains returned.

With the fervor of a zealot, a man in a pair of
sunglasses
mimed his way out of a box.
A few attache-holders stopped and watched.
Even fewer gave money to his visible box,
grimmed by the oily street.

"I will not go back," said someone from the
crowd.
A scent of sauteed onions clung to the air.
A woman in a dress began to pirouette
like a confident, beginner dancer.
A man looked up.

The turnpike collapsed with no one on it.
Some zwieback bread fell out a car window.
The tall birds dispersed. A new crowd in
torpedo crowns
and T-shirts appeared in the cosmopolitan
commons.
They looked around then left abruptly.

IV

Stillness is the gateway rug to bliss.

Fortunes will come in the form of car parts.
It holds together,
it really does:
a dove.

Self-rule is the new way, the old way, the way.
The fire of youth is a blind hunger.

Its use is to burn, it does not distinguish
between appropriate and undeserving. So
self-rule is the fruit of seven-figure experience
points, as experience points.

Swaraj is the Sanskrit word for self-rule.
Teachers teach through redundancy-laced
variation.
The swaraj soul is always vigilant, always on the
lookout for freedom.
Defining freedom limits freedom.
Freedom is not just the freedom to shop.

How can I continue in a cage?
I count my breaths.
I count the chips in the whited bricks.
I stop counting to close my eyes.
My eyes.

Love is the constitution of life.
Everything moves.
Protection is a natural preservative.
The martial arts accompany the marital arts.
Your eyes.

Arithmetic is an exclusive language among
a million languages.
Initiation into a secret elitism must be met with
a solidified solitude.
Those with peepholes are people.

Eyes.

In the beginning was the AUM. Swaraj is a
sonorous sound.
As it all spirals from one center, serpent and
bird merge into man.
The species with the least possessions is the
most evolved.
Listen to them all, even the people without
eyes.

V

"I can hear it," said Gladys as gold skyscrapers
levitated
above the docks made of unpublished books
and first drafts.
The sea looked up at the second horizon.
The sky looked
into the core of the Earth with a Superman-like
gaze.
"Free."

A symphony of droning-augmented disarray
breathed from several boomboxes
positioned near the street vendor's cash
registers.
A line formed to buy hot dogs.
A tree appeared on TV.
The wind moved its branches.

Growth is determined by cryptic creodes.
Oaths are hard to remain true to. It can be
done.

"I want to grow," said Wally Four Feathers.
Turtles emerged from the sand with a languaged
cadence.
Free as a mom.

"If you are born into life, you hold the death card.
Be accountable," said Bill Affinity.
He was like a bull without being a bully.
He was aligned with self-rule. He was free.
He is still free.

VI

A neutrino passes through lead unhindered.
A neutrino is the threading agent
bringing catalytic elixirs to the element lead,
transforming it into gold.
A neutrino walks like a native pioneer into the
plenum.

The five senses convolve to spin a suchness.
"I want to take out the trash," says Besty McValue.
Besty likes a consortium of beasts
so frees them from the local imperial menagerie
whenever they show up.
Besty and Bill spend money,
but not Monad's money.
Clarabell avoids Gladys
until Gladys finds the wherewithal to simplify like
she used to before the flood.

Wally Four Feathers is a father of interstellar
constitutions.
The rich ore found on Chiron's invisible moon,
Samsonalia
(which was also discovered by human beings
in 1977),
is largely made of selenite, an integral
component used
in the threading of lead by neutrinos to change
it into gold.

Someone with a knack for surfboard
hydrodynamics
actually made the galactic cut and philosopher-
stoned lead into gold with his eyes tied behind
his back
while drinking sea water
from an unknown subterranean sea on Venus.

Language can be baggage. A cabbage can
unspool into a creode.

A student with perfect attendance for hooky
can play hockey
with a hooker's hickey if he has a doctor's note
and a green pen with the doctor's thumbprint
on it to prove it. All is well in Macedonia.

Lambasted, the window washers in Ethiopia
will take a shorter lunch break until they feel
behooved

by the spice found in the coating on their
chicken nuggets.
"I like rock and roll," says Besty to Bill.
Bill turns the radio up. The radio plays
'The Question' by The Moody Blues.

VII

Prepare to begin again. Prepare a solitude.
Look outside
the window at the black diamond asphalt of the
twilight street. Make a drink. Drink that drink.
Prepare for a hangover and make another drink.
Memorize a memorandum.

"I wish I had a Pepto Bismol-like tonic for the
ears on my rhododendron," said the radio in a
thick Slavic accent. A hot dog vendor
expired with a smile on his unshaven face.
Lightning struck the beach. Slowly lowering his
memorandum, Frank smiled. The sky rained
gold, chanting, "Continuum."

"I have it," said Wally to Clarabell and her
friend, Moss. The gritty sidewalk turned green.
"Adventure!" yelled Moss.
Stoic landscapes held stature until the rains
completed their dharma.
"Well, *I* had it... " said a disconcerted Clarabell.

Monad was throwing a fit.
Somehow someone stole all his money and
replaced it with
exact replicas. Or so it seemed. And then
a gust of fire inverted and became like a
hovering, bifurcating water. Everybody stopped
chattering, stopped clapping for attention,

stopped brushing wet tresses of multi-ethnic
hair from their cheekbones. A tree grew at an
incredibly fast pace
from beneath the asphalt in the middle of the
busy street. All the cars skidded and rested.
The city banks exploded like pinatas, scattering
legal tender

all over the industrial tourism. A song began.
It was new. Or so it seemed. The lyrics were in
Esperanto:
Angelo kun glavo, preta...
But the chorus was in Indian and English
tongues simultaneously:
Swaraj...

Abigail,

I love you.

—Michael

Fasting

Auburn fern
lathering stallion
desiccated desert
quartz medallion

A fist of leaves laid dry
before infernal rogation
before slow sun's swanning rotation
through square season station

promulgated fossil lace
cream and cadmium corpse
veinface
rockrace

Stone ground
bone
Bone ground
stone

Slowing

Roiling turquoise
tidal hand
susurrus silvers scroll the land
sibilating the silent sand

With the hydrogen lead of floating nostalgia
she
levied a balance
ballooning night bathing

Eight to one
won
one in eight
Hoodoo wee ape rishi ate

Resin
gloves squeak
treasonable
trait

Somnambulist

Fowl fishing through opposing throngs for
scintilli
for the serpent of faith
the supramundane coiled cracked garden hose
the horse zen
a bowl of blue bowels

then children then women then men

Weighty meatballs cutting their teeth
on red radiant saws

Waif thief
"Lethe, wait!"

way

Abigail Lewis,

I LOVE YOU ALWAYS FOREVER ETERNALLY

—Michael Louis Mollo

BLM

Blossom Lady May
This ground down gourd pound
this multifoliate ground
is love profound
the boon unbound

It
lathes in lithe lamping
her moxious muscle mood

"Dude, truce!"
deucedly poofed by big pig
love's uprooted tuber animated by apogee intel
a centillion times faster than
the average bird bay bee AI
Shirl's trip ship
not spot on no not a bit bid fin
fed blip
bled dead blimp head arid

Fortified

Castles were made of stone
not only to keep the enemy out,
but allow the warrior within
to destroy his own chattel
as often as he had to
without affecting
the integrity of the structure.

AL,

Do you know how much I love you?
More than that.

—MLM

The Constitution of God

Love.

Why the Beast Haunts Man

Zoos.

Swag

Club cred cried:
"A wrecktriangle
is an eggsample
of eggsackedness!"

Abigail Lewis,

Merry Christmas and a Happy New Year
and a perfect forever
for you
with you
my dear wife

I love you

—Michael Louis Mollo

Two Years Silent

Hitchhike

at one
with the
angel of presence

warm wind
thick hair
loose stance

boots shift

highway hiss

give yourself an emptiness

M + A = Everlasting Love

Under Endyein Dusk

And moonlight; aye, to all the mazy world
—John Keats, *Endymion*

Polaris, I am sorry if I hurt you. The bee-trayore
in U needs to stop. Ewe need to stop. Haul.
Putting down the sheep. Stop. Asia.
—Badee Billee

I
Roaring
waves
crash
against
sea-rock

below.
Above,
ruins.
Stark
temples

twined with garlands of cobalt morning
glory and bramble: an entrance, and under
endyein dusk, a lion.
"He… is… not p-p-putting up with…
y-your inamorata's… k-katas," said Fillipe
Pepe Felicia Goodbuy, "Am-m-mazing maize,
corn is."

II
Carbolic
sky rolls
over bro-
ken Corinth-
ian columns,

rain
comes
down.
The
marble

lion is maned. Chips of rock slip from
moonlit piles.
"Apollymi!"
There never was an answer. "Sher Apollymi!"
Old old old old night.
"Ma! Maaa!"

III
Cracked,
the cat's
mouth—
a thick bronze
lock.

IV
The catacomb key clicks,
old stone-on-stone grinds loose, an ancient door
opens.
Fallow,
yellow dust ascends through the epic ephemeral
illuminings of a roaring sky's lightning lashings.
Momentarily,

a glowing placarded script appears:
Λαβύρινθος του Λιονταριού. Blackened,
then golden, the archway inscription plate,
now pale, is wreathed with stone rosettes,
half-paisley from lichens: *Lavýrinthos tou
Liontarioú.* This daunting caterwauls in
translucency a whisper of ardent ardor for
universal Grecian

mazes–masias; classically calculated Greek,
Alexandrian, and modern mind-topography:
Codex Alexandrinus, Masias; Codex Vaticanus,
Meisaias; Sher Apollymi/Badee
Billee.

V

...as more strident horses arrive. "I am looking
up at the sky and it is

gravely in-"
The Principality of Catalonia when ruled by the

Crown of Aragon,
Bragon, Cragon,
Dragon.

...stut stut stut stut stut stut stut stut stut stut
stut stut
grim mimminings and LO! smithsonite delight
tonight right bite fi-
"Did you evacuate the premise? Did you- oh,
shut the fuck up–did you tit?"
– mythological Greece in spectral *Panthera leo*
persica
Lalaism

collage:
Labyrinth of the
Lion.
Steps lead down.
Up.

MTT

Abby,

I just want you to know
how grateful I am for you
in my life. I look around
at all the beautiful abundance
making this a happy house.
Thank you for the countless
good things you do.
I love you.

—Michael

*Do you know how much I love
you? Yes, you don't.
More, much more than that. Hi.*

M heart A

Standing on the Roof

Enough of these sybaritic pseudo-bards
vomiting violence; enough
of the stacks of cash shaken at jiggling asses
in gold chains. Sugar,

all you need is
a measure of decency
and self-restraint, a dollop of virtue,
a taste of taste.

Compassion distilled from pain.
Character beyond pride
for blotted gauze and juiced zippers.
Love

of wilderness is where truth begins.
Still, the blood-orange smog of promising LA
holds esoteric thermals of intense creativity.
People have a chance among Angels.

The only other option
is cans of broken graffiti
and a chipped plate of
nihilism.

Can you make me a food?

The Dream of Phil

"Sally-Go-Wild was her name,
and she spun ideas like a lazy Susan.
We had pepper from Greenwich Village
tossed with saffron from Kashmir.

We had capicola from Genoa
slapped with cheese from Nice.
We had arbitration from Ukraine's
collection of suitcases

mingled with Japanese mittens.
We had one die
and a thousand pips
to see.

We had straw from Bedouin canteen straps
flying into hazmat suit breast plate insignias.
The art splash of un-adroit
modernism

made way
for a return
to discipline,"
his dream said.

Fresh

Taking a breath on psilocybin
was like a stellar bellows
with basketball cheeks.

Smiling for hours
induced lactic acid
to athleticise a mouth's sociophysiology.

Eyes were benevolent shark slate.
Clothes hung like Usnea.
Flintstone feet made the body carriage carry.

Then the wit found its whet stone and whey.
Gazelles roamed without worry of predation
through plains on Shanghai strip mall rooftops.

Aghast before altars of muddy onyx,
Wally read his palm for protocols.
Wally's proxy parachuted off an agrarian visor,

lifting momentarily like a seeding
dandelion orb seed
and whisker consortium.

And night popped cosmic spheres
across the billiard table
inverting its Schopenhauer museum

back into place
redundantly until recalcitrant pheromones
delighted into day.

It's okay...

Abigail Lewis,

Sweet love, I want to thank you for hanging in there with me. You are my dream come true. You are so many perfect and beautiful things, like a June tree blazing with a multitude of diverse, virtuous leaves.

I love you. Now and forever. We have such a blessed life with Fleuffer. I am eternally grateful.

Merry Christmas and a happy new year to my glorious, sacred wife. And happy anniversary.

—Michael Louis Mollo

Happy Birthday
Abigail
I LOVE YOU!!!

Love, Michael

HCoVRI

Vibrant

I see you
as you extend your hand
to touch the wisteria.

You make tea
and serve platters of food
to orient the guest.

There is tenderness—
whorls of fingertip on velvet,
talking to the cats.

There is joy—
a quick jig to the song bridge
under carmine crow's feet of sunset.

There is stillness—
a shawl of silence,
breathing the tides of time.

Nice?
Not nice?
Nice.

Conspiracy

Ravens caw
like opium
crones,

ravens
the color
of shaman hair.

Ravens
reach ruddy
in old pale bones,

and loosely
level the
air.

Kaua

The Key Lion

And fiery demons all dance when you walk
through that door

Don't say you're easy on me, you're about as easy
as a nuclear war
—Duran Duran, *Is There Something I Should*
Know

Huh?
—Zhang Xichun

I

A line of oval lights hill-climbing, hell-
climbing, 4 th of Jewel-Eye Phthalo blue
avuncular greening,
seer in NVG, Magi epiphany aspiring spiral short
snort–
A trust A fly A-frame

"Are you jazzed?" she asked.
"I like it when I am out of-" I said.
"Hey!" MenManyMerryChance DeliberateNamo

II

The Key Lion
Da qi line in deign decline, "Recall your first
smile with her."
We ham are X-pressing 455 new ways to weigh
this old Just-
inian procedure... to decide, to not, to let, to force,

to confuse, to fu se, to be, to kick, to chart, to
kites: you r fly. To cllude ;; oo
To produce, to maim, to claim, to roost.
Hoo   t   t o r e s t i n r e d f o r e styes

No, to be-
no,
2   ttime

III

After much introspection, Shams-i-Tabrizi,
 I must conclude.
There an array of disposters – one two three
and on it is on good on
No more, she qualled.
"I have it! I have it!" Nomenclature. Gnome's
Domes. A Nome day plume. Syllogistically,
we've woven thrice o'er; moved on–it is good.

 Good. oarnky can't

"Why do Chinese sages have horns in those
old depictions?" she asked. "Because TED Talks
are of a dark platform," he said, lifting his clear
Starbucks cup.

Fuck you,
there will be music, poetry, divination;
there will be this;
there will be that.
Angry Big Cat.

IV

Burning bushido budo Pluto poo-uno,
Dodo *and don't put down the Dodo!*
Human goat **Hanuman** urinating on
the White House lawn nightly.

You paisley tie
tit mouse lice house,
wedding rice and crotch rocket wannabe,
Newbie Fred.

Agrariatarian

Two.

+

Abigail,

I LOVE YOU

— Michael
How wonderful you are! Have a great day.

Abigail Lewis,

Thank you for remaining true
to yourself.

And thank you for:
- Taking such good care of me
- Making me good food
- Cleaning up after me
- Finding me doctors
- Being patient with me (no pun)
- Being present
- Always making sure I have smoke
- Great road trips
- Sharing intimate personal growth
- Forgiving me
- Trusting me
- Having faith in me
- Hearing me
- Being there for so many
- Caring
- Supporting my art
- Honoring your parents
- Finding me such a special place to live
- Allowing me to care for you
- Remaining strong
- Allowing me to be strong
- Confiding in me
- Thanksgiving at my camp
- Christmas every year
- All the little things I missed

- All the little things I didn't miss
- In short, thank you

I honor you
I love you
I love you

— Michael

Abigail,

I love you.

— Michael

Abigail,

Your light is great. I am truly impacted, impressed, and inspired to champion my own life because of your example.

You have clearly and honorably served so many in their endeavors without asking for very much. I think it is time others supported your undertakings… now!!!

Thank you, dear dear friend of many.

— Michael

Abigail,

You are the best! I cleaned the house the best I could w/out vacuummmming. Best.

I love you.

— Michael

Knowing

Knowing history
matters not—

know virtue
and write

your own
good story.

Hi Love,

I love you.

Love, Michael

Cantillation

Roll the rock
from this tomb.

A gyre of gypsies
doxologizes the moon.

Maverick as sulphur,
they enter the room

yet chantey this shanty
 its imminent boon.

A,

Have a great day. I Love You!!!!

— M

Of Myth and Man
(An Auspice in Trochaic Trimeter)

You, in wake of eagle
feathers fanning Heaven,
furiously regal,
generation seven,

your destiny's been weighed,
no, not by careful men,
but by the birds of prey
stoking Armageddon.

Equus stands on your soil,
on theirs he leaves his breath:
conqueror of royal men
and literal myth.

Abigail, Welcome Home.

— MM

Coronation

Viridian leaf
above the tears

wreaths even the belt
beyond the spheres,

bests winking platters
of polished fears;

verdigris for vacuity
when no one hears:

a crown of laurel
for the years.

M heart A

Homage

You are everything
beautiful, courageous, wise—
wind in whorling grass.

Abigail,

I love you.

— Michael

Trees

Nature and qi
and the character of things

sovereign

It is absolute
a reverence and a union

*Today you will have
the best day you've ever had.
Tomorrow, better.*

Cha-O-Ha

The Lakota warrior
still on the hill
still looking
still

Far Away Camp

Bottom Line

Motley splendor striding
through dark squalor

pulling prize husks
from wet garbage

together
and

like
you

the street freaks
are still concerned

wholly
with love

Love honor, honor love.

Easy

The same tree
has made seed

Relax into
your ever-highness

What pains you
what stains you

washes away
like watercolor in rain

It rises
away

The sun gives you
again this day

Greatness

You

Strategy

Yes, to think ahead
for seven generations
before making moves.

You get only one chance every moment.

Word

I read *Discover* magazine
and *Men's Health*,
both generally gorked
regarding speciesism,

a beginner Bodhisattva's
dime-driven diatribe
avoiding arboreal bionics.
Even the editorials.

A dog bounds
through five desert rings,
five mysteries. His caller,
a Yo-Yo Ma Sha Na Na.

Then
The New Yorker:
Too many commas,
too many clips.

Less plastic, more petrichor.
Less choo-choo, more cha-cha.

Conch

And then I tide back
into this shore's density,
a storehouse of bifurcations,
a yacht of ultimatums;

a clumsying of yucca spears
dulled to disproportion;
falling raven feathers
palming a votical egg

into the spore of inversion,
into a black hole zygote.
"Hello," the free man says
to the Olympic soothsayer.

Silence triages the succession
of concrete curbs broken back
into assuming acumen
of mortared gravel.

Only sidereal declination
can shift the blindness now
that capillary diaphanousness
exhilarates at the aura-end of spring trees.

And then off to sleep again,
this time without the assumption
that dream world is secondary.
You move, that is all.

Then roll your sugar bowl contents out
like phosphorous geodes
onto the shellacked ebony
of creode runway.

A spool hibernating from frayed fluff,
splayed stuff.
The uninterrogated gambol
of voicey teethings. Bullseye

fruition chiming from disked obelisk.
Mountain the formless, the singularization,
the polarized divisioning, the multiplicity.
The Arc de Triomphe

as, initially, a rabbit's zig-zaggy return
to the rooty warren,
later fulminating as procedural bubble
obfuscated by its own solubility.

Dubstep bread flattened
to fit under
the cell door.
He pipes up,

"The occult became
outlawed when the outlaw
became occulted."
Tangerines served on leaf springs,

halved and drizzled
with honeyed prickly pear water.
The smell of rust.

"Tandem."

Sycan

How the West Was One

How the west was one
was in our faces,
in our hearts
hearthed in our heaven-honeyed souls,

as its magma music erupted
from that platinum Honda Civic zephyr
like a psychedelic paroxysm
for elite etheric lights,

for wild royalty,
for rogue alpha pairs.
We were the king and queen
of all sentient beings,

of all things in existence
and non-existence
eternally protected
by empyrean love;

all things were coupled as binary
sun-sugared pears
as we cascaded down highway 395
high.

I remember how you looked
in my mother's blue denim dress,
the one my grandmother had made for her, and
how I thought you were a living monument

to the manifestation of three wishes in one
as we kissed and blissed
on the velvet herb, sharing a peace pipe
made of what might as well have been
Alexandrian glass.

The same faithful winds
would see us set sail in snow
listening to Bob Dylan's best, then later
Let It Be and *Ten*
by your sacred spot in verdant spring twilight.

I remember feeling a power in purity
aligned with the free wolves of the wilderness
as we saw that lone wolf look at us, turn,
and run
on Indian Road.

I remember thinking
all the cliches
as "a dream came true"
when "I found my soul mate".

Thank you, Love.

An Hour

An hour of birds
inter-winters loess and tripe,
wicking sustenance
through clear membranes
on frozen flowers,
still silts.

Love tough

Praise

Did you do your characters
justice?

No amount of writing
could describe a human soul,

yet one prayer to The Maker
resounds.

I honor you, Love.

Dearest Abigail,

Happy Birthday.
One moon away.
My love for you:
limitless, eternal.

Love, Michael

I'll see you again.

Twilight Song

And now the sky calls to you
I'm flying from this far edge too

Oh baby why must you take so long
From the misty woods a twilight song

And now the sky calls to me
Let us all fly forever free

Oh baby I won't be long
From the misty woods a twilight song

GOD
Mother Mary
Jesus Christ

Acknowledgements

I would like to thank with all my heart my MOST AMAZING mother, Sandi, father, Daniel, sister, Jennifer, sister, Jessie, brother, Christopher, relatives and friends for their great love and support. I would also like to thank, of course, my faithful wife, Abigail, and her wonderful family, Chris, Anna, and Toby Lewis. Gratitude is extended also to poets John Trudell, Sylvia Plath, Jim Morrison, and Amanda Lovelace for their beautiful influences. I am most honored to have worked with Chris Molé in getting this book published.

About the Author

Michael Louis Mollo was born in the Los Angeles area. At age twenty-three he decided to pursue life as a poet in the wilderness— experiencing homelessness in forty-five American cities. Asceticism, fasting, and two years of silence, while being forced into jails and psychiatric institutions, are chronicalized through his poetry.

At age thirty-five, Michael met Abigail. During their sixteen years together, Abby helped Michael regain his balance. Michael expresses his journey through poetry, music and painting.